Stop Taking My Things

by Jan Weeks

illustrated by Janine Dawson

The Characters

Tim

Mandy

Mum

The Setting

CONTENTS

Chapter 1
Tim the Terror! 2

Chapter 2
Find and Destroy! 8

Chapter 3
Tim the Troublemaker . . 14

Chapter 4
The Plan 20

Chapter 5
The Better Plan 32

CHAPTER

Tim the Terror!

I have this little brother.
His name is Tim.
Mum wants me to like him
but I don't.

He takes all my toys.
Then he breaks them.

It all started when Tim
was a baby. He couldn't talk
but he made loud "Give me!" noises.

"Waaaahhhhh," he yells
when he wants one of my things.

When I don't give it to him,
he screams louder.

"He won't hurt it," Mum says.
"Let Tim have a turn."

It was even worse
when Tim learnt to crawl.
Down the hall he'd go
on his fat little hands and knees,
straight into my bedroom.

CHAPTER

Find and Destroy!

One day I found Tim sitting on my bedroom floor chewing my teddy bear's nose. He was dribbling all over it.

Another day he took my best doll and pulled out one of its arms and most of its hair.
Then he said the doll was his when I took it back.

Tim yelled so loudly that Mum came running into the room.

"What have you done to him?" Mum asked me.

"Be nice to your little brother," she said as she cuddled Tim. "He's only a baby."

When Tim started to walk,
things got even worse.
Nothing was safe. Not my books!
Not my toys! Not anything!

"He'll grow out of it," Mum said.

He didn't.

Tim the Troublemaker

One day, Tim took my homework out of my school bag.
He tore out all the pages
and ripped them into little pieces.

"I'm making snow," he said, as he threw the pieces over his head.

So I didn't do my homework.
My teacher was cross
when I told her what had happened
to my book. But she wasn't mad
at Tim. She was cross with me.

"You must learn
to take more care, Mandy,"
she said. "Don't leave your things
where your little brother
can get them."

Where could that be?

I was getting really tired of Tim.
I had to think of a way
to keep him out of my bedroom.

There was no use putting a
"KEEP OUT TIM!" sign
on the door. Tim couldn't read.
I had to think of something else.

CHAPTER

The Plan

Finally, I came up with a plan.
I could hardly wait to try it out.

"I have a secret," I whispered into Tim's ear. Of course he wanted to know what it was.

"There is a hungry monster with sharp teeth living under my bed," I told him. "It's a great big, hairy monster that only eats little boys called Tim."

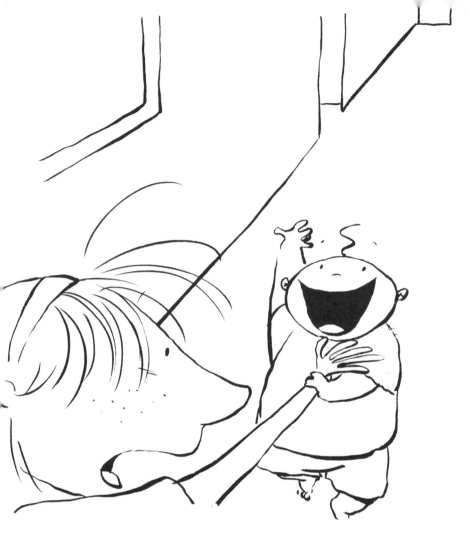

"Show me," Tim said.
He began to drag me down the hall.
Some kids don't know that
you should be scared of monsters.

There was no monster under my bed so I said, "Sssh, he's sleeping. We'll come back later."

I had to think of a better plan.

Today I found Tim sitting in my bedroom again. He was drawing all over one of the school's new library books.

"This is my drawing of a house," he said, smiling at me.
"I drew it for you, Mandy."

"Now I'm going to get into big trouble with Mrs Potts!" I yelled. "And she's the crankiest teacher in the whole school."

Tim put his arms around me. "I'm sorry," he said, showing me his sorry face.

It was a bit late for that.
I pushed him away. Then I told him
to get out of my bedroom
and stay out!

Chapter 5

The Better Plan

That afternoon, my friend, Paul, came over.

Paul liked my new plan. "The table tennis balls make great eyes," Paul said.

We were sitting in my bedroom turning Mum's mop into a monster.

It was going to be Paul's job to hide under the bed and be the monster. When I brought Tim into the room, Paul would roar.

When Tim got close enough,
Paul the Monster
was going to grab Tim's ankle.

It was a good plan
but it didn't work.

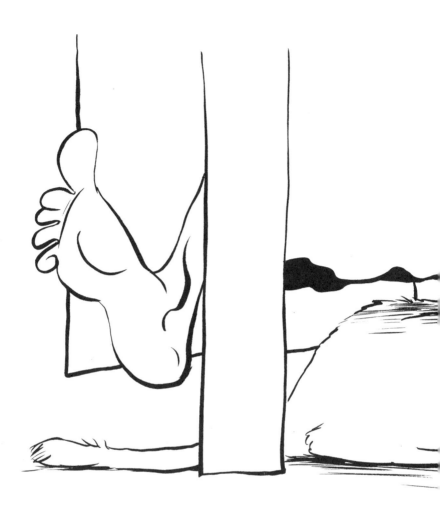

I didn't plan on the cat being asleep under my bed.
And I didn't plan on Tim standing on the cat's tail.

The cat let out such a wail that I was the one who ended up getting the fright.

As I stepped back, I tripped over the mop. I landed on the floor and hurt my arm.

Now I've thought
of an even better plan.

I'm going to ask Grandma
if she'd like Tim to live with her.
I hope she says yes.

GLOSSARY

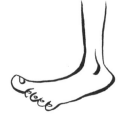

ankle
the joint where your foot meets your leg

crankiest
the angriest

cross
angry

cuddled
gave a big hug

destroy
wreck or break

terror
a big fright

wail
a loud cry

worse
more than bad

Jan Weeks

How high can you jump?
> That depends on what's chasing me. A snake would make me jump very high. A spider would make me jump even higher.

Why do ants have 6 legs?
> Ants have two legs at either end of their body to stop them falling over and two more in the middle to use as spares.

What is your favourite toy?
> Our new boat.

What is the hardest part of your day?
> Surviving in city traffic.

Janine Dawson

How high can you jump?
> It depends how high I am in the tree.

Why do ants have 6 legs?
> Because if they had 7 they'd limp.

What is your favourite toy?
> My daughter, my cats and cardboard boxes.

What is the hardest part of your day?
> Actually sitting at my desk to start work.